KNIGHTS

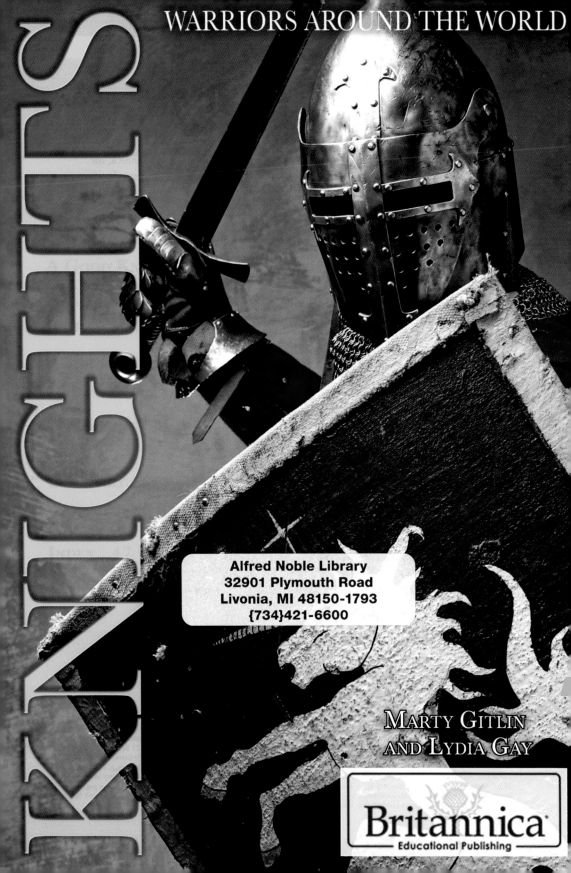

WARRIORS AROUND THE WORLD

KNIGHTS

MARTY GITLIN
AND LYDIA GAY

Britannica
Educational Publishing

INTRODUCTION

Stories of knights and knighthood have been passed down for centuries. Movies and television depictions have strengthened the legend of the most significant military figures of the Middle Ages.

One envisions knights as warriors mounted on horses and dressed in suits of armor. That view is more or less accurate. The word "knight" is derived from the Old English word *cniht*, the equivalent of the Latin word *caballarius*, meaning "horseman." And they did indeed wear suits of armor, chain mail, or hardened leather for protection. They also carried weapons, such as swords and lances.

Knights arose as a distinct order around the year 1000. The first knights appeared in France. They were typically young men from noble families or from non-noble families that owned land and property (called landed gentry). Their roles as warriors and as protectors of royalty often earned them titles of lordship and property.

The ideal knight of the Middle Ages was gallant, virtuous, and brave and was sworn to protect those who could not protect

themselves. This idealistic behavior became known as the chivalric code. Images of chivalrous knights rescuing damsels in distress and protecting the downtrodden were popularized and cemented by the literature of that period and beyond. In reality, however, many knights did not live up to these expectations.

The era of knighthood emerged and thrived before guns and gunpowder forever changed military strategy. Knights first appeared

Many people today are fascinated by knights and the Middle Ages. Some of these people have created and joined groups dedicated to re-creating medieval culture, crafts, and skills. Here, two such men participate in a late-medieval-style joust.

This illustration from the early thirteenth century Codex Manesse *shows a knight and his squire. The squire cares for his master's horse as the knight prepares to fight.*

his knight into battle to aid in the conflict should his lord be out-matched and to lend his horse should his master lose his own. The squire also had the distasteful duty of picking up a fallen knight or removing him from the field of battle if he had been killed or wounded.

Practicing to become a knight required tremendous skill and repetition in various military arts, such as the proper use of the lance and sword both on horseback and on foot. Squires spent several hours a day learning to ride horses and fight. It took years for squires to master effective use of weaponry while galloping on horseback. A squire would begin his training by riding ponies and fighting with wooden weapons before he graduated to a horse and real blades. He learned to carry a lance and practiced jousting by thrusting lances through a wooden ring hung from a rope as he sped by on horseback. He was taught to properly care for horses and to train horses for battle.

But warfare training was only one aspect of a squire's education. He also learned to read and write, acquired basic math skills, and was taught the essential tenants of Christian theology. And a knight-in-training was versed in courtly manners. His time as a page and squire taught him the customs and rituals of court life and he was also exposed to tales of chivalry. Some of these tales were written down, but most people in the Middle Ages heard them told aloud by travelling players and troubadours. These chivalric stories told of knights who exercised modesty and self-control despite their physical strength and power.

Arthur's knights, including Lancelot and Galahad, depart on a quest. Lancelot was a noble but flawed knight. Galahad was the knightly ideal.

I Dub Thee...

Squires who performed well eventually became knights. Early knighting ceremonies were rather simple: a noble bestowed the arms and rank of knight upon his successful squire. Over time the dubbing ceremonies became increasingly elaborate. They involved solemn vows and religious sanction. The honored began by taking a purification bath, then kneeling or standing all night in prayer before an altar on which lay the armor he would don the next day. A sermon followed in the morning in

The ceremony reached its crescendo in the courtyard of the lord's castle. In the presence of the assembled knights and ladies, pages buckled the armor on the new knight piece by piece, girded a sword about his waist, and attached spurs to his feet. The young man then knelt before the officiating lord or knight, usually the knight who had trained him. Using the flat of his sword or his fist, the officiant lightly struck the young man upon the neck or shoulder, officially dubbing him a knight.

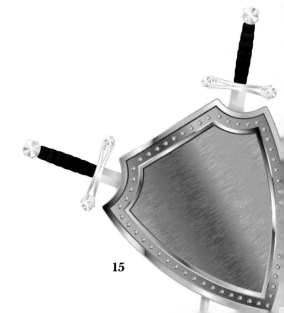

15

Chapter 2
Fighting for Show

I t did not take long for a new knight to start his most popular activity: competing in tournaments. Many knights participated in such events immediately following their dubbing ceremonies. These competitions were designed to show off the knights' fighting skills, as well as their courage.

In the mêlée, two opposing groups of knights fought each other on horseback and on foot. Mêlées were mock battles, but knights could still be badly injured or killed.

Medieval tournaments consisted of jousts between two knights or battles between groups, called mêlées. Knights, new and established, would converge from miles around to entertain the hosting court, their guests, and the local peasants. Sometimes the visitors came in such numbers that the lodgings of the castle were filled and tents were erected to accommodate the late arrivals. Medieval literature describes tournament knights dressed in shining and resplendent armor, with pages and squires carrying each knight's banner.

Tournaments generally began after morning mass and could last for a single day or extend for several. Although the events in a tournament were meant to be nonlethal contests, the challenges were still extremely dangerous. Tournament knights used blunted weapons, but the sport was so rough and the knights jousted with such passion that many were wounded and some were even killed.

17

THE MOUNTED JOUST

One of the most iconic events in a medieval tournament was the mounted joust with lance. The rules and procedures of this event, as well as the other tournament events, changed greatly over the course of the Middle Ages. But by the late medieval period the rules for the mounted joust had generally codified as follows: two opponents, each riding a horse and carrying a lance, faced each other across as field. The knights then galloped toward each other, pointing their lances at the opponent. As the knights met, each tried to strike the other with his lance;

The mounted joust with lance is probably the most well-known tournament event. This illustration from 1448 shows two knights, John Chalon of England and Lois de Beul of France, jousting in front of an audience of nobles.

if the lance did hit a knight it would often splinter and break. The knights repeated this course for a predetermined number of runs, or until one of the knights was knocked off his horse. If one of the knights was unhorsed during a joust, he automatically lost the contest and was forced to yield his horse and armor to the winner. If neither was unhorsed, then the knight who struck the most hits won the competition.

A COSTLY SPORT

Competing in tournaments was expensive. Even for these contests knights needed horses trained for war, called chargers and destriers. Common mares and work-horses would have been terrified by the sounds of lances shattering and crashing armor. Warhorses were specially trained to charge into battle and ignore the frightening sounds of combat. By the end of the thirteenth century such a horse could cost as much as half a year's salary for a knight.

Armor was another substantial expense. Early knights donned chain mail shirts that extended to their knees, a helmet with a nose guard, and carried round shields. Plate armor suits, made of iron or steel, eventually replaced linked chain mail. Suits of armor better protected knights from most

A GREAT KNIGHT OF BRITAIN

William Marshal was one of the most respected knights of medieval England. Born around 1146, he was the younger son of a minor noble. As a youth, he was sent to Normandy where he was trained and eventually knighted by the Chamberlain of Normandy in 1166. He competed regularly in tournaments throughout Europe for several years after his knighting, where he made a very good living and earned renown as one of the most successful tournament knights of the day. During this time Marshal also began training the eldest living son of King Henry II of England, Henry, known as the Young King.

In 1173, young Henry, along with two of his brothers and his mother, led a revolt against Henry II. William Marshal supported young Henry during this conflict, serving as a military

The effigy from the tomb of William Marshal. Marshal was buried in Temple Church in London, England.

leader. When the revolt failed in 1174, young Henry and his brothers returned to their father's service and were welcomed back to court, as was Marshal. He continued to serve young Henry until the Young King's death in 1183. After two years fighting with the Knights Templar in the Holy Land, Marshal returned to serve Henry II directly, as well as his successor, King Richard I.

Under Richard I's rule Marshal was granted a prosperous marriage and given the title Earl of Pembroke. When Richard departed for the Third Crusade in 1190, he made Marshal a member of the council of regency. This council was responsible for running the kingdom while Richard was away.

After the death of Richard I, Marshal served Richard's brother and successor, King John. Although the two had a temporary falling out, Marshal continued to support King John through his difficult reign. Many of the other English nobles were unhappy with John's rule and led a rebellion against him. Marshal did not support John's treatment of the nobles, but he stayed loyal to the king throughout the civil war. Because of this he was respected by both sides.

Following the death of King John, Marshal was chosen by his peers in England as regent for John's nine-year-old son, Henry III. While regent, and at age seventy, Marshal ended the civil war at the Battle of Lincoln. He died on May 14, 1219. He is still considered the epitome of knighthood and chivalry.

Plate armor like this protected knights against swords and lances but was still vulnerable to arrows and spears.

swords and lances. Helmets also became longer and heavier, completely covering the head and neck with slits for the eyes and for breathing.

At tournament a knight might lose his horse and armor, so he needed to have extras in reserve or enough money to buy new ones if he wanted to keep competing. Finally, he needed to keep and maintain weapons, including a sword and several lances (which were purposefully broken and replaced in mounted jousts).

In true battles, outside of the tournaments, knights might be taken prisoner by the opposing army. In such cases the knight or his family had to pay ransom to attain his freedom.

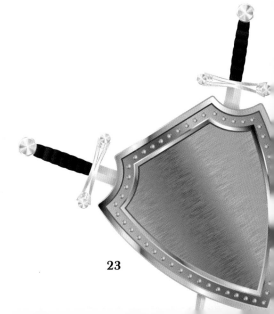

CHAPTER 3
THE LIFE OF A KNIGHT

Knights made their living with their military skills. After his dubbing, a young knight had to find a way to support himself. Those who could often returned to their father's castle to serve their family and eventually inherit. However, knights who were younger sons or whose fathers had only small estates could not depend on their family or an inheritance for a living. Called knights-errant, these men had to travel through Europe to find a lord who would accept them as a vassal or to compete in tournaments and make a living from any winnings. Many knights, both errant and pledged, also chose to join one of the many crusades that were waged in the Holy Land or in the Christian reconquest of Spain. And some knights, whose lords decided to join a crusade, were compelled to join as well.

FIGHTING FOR REAL

Any knight pledged to the king, or pledged to a lord who was the vassal of the king, was obliged to go to war at the king's command. They sometimes paid the king to avoid military service. That money was then used to hire battle-tested mercenaries. Many knights, however, proved to be brave and willing soldiers.

Medieval wars were waged in a combination of small-scale clashes between groups of knights and large-scale pitched battles. In an army, knights were divided into units, each with ten to twenty knights

The armies of England and France fight each other at the battle of Crécy. Note the infantrymen who are fighting on foot rather than on horseback. Medieval armies had many more infantrymen than knights.

Archers became an important part of medieval armies. England was particularly well known for skilled archers. This battle scene between English and Spanish armies shows the English using their famous long-bowmen before the opposing knights charge each other.

and a commander. During war these units might fight planned or impromptu skirmishes. Large battles between opposing armies included many units of knights as well as infantry foot soldiers and archers, particularly longbowmen.

CHIVALRY LIVES ON?

Regardless of where or who a knight served, medieval society expected him to follow certain rules of behavior. By the thirteenth century, knights were guided by the motto "Religion, Honor, and Courtesy." They were expected to fight bravely in battle and to remain loyal to their lord and lady, as well as to be pious, modest, and well-mannered.

The medieval poet Chaucer described an ideal knight: "And though he was valorous, he was prudent and as meek as a maid of his bearing. In all his life he never yet spake discourteously but was truly a perfect gentle knight." The gallantry and honor alluded to by Chaucer was known as chivalry, from the French word for knight, "chevalier."

Not every knight, however, lived up to these standards. The rules of chivalry stated that knights must protect and defend women and children and never prey upon merchants, peasants, or clergy. Nevertheless, some knights took advantage of their superior strength and the breakdown

A page from Chaucer's Canterbury Tales, *which has an illumination of Chaucer's ideal knight*

A FINE KNIGHT OF FRANCE

Jean II le Maingre, nicknamed Boucicaut, exemplified the ideals of chivalry. After becoming a knight at age sixteen he served King Charles VI of France in several

A fifteenth-century engraving of Jean II le Maingre, known as Boucicaut

military campaigns, and was appointed a marshal of France in 1391. Boucicaut was famous in his time for exceptional military dedication and for an extreme training program that was far beyond what most knights did. From 1384 and 1391 he successfully fought in three Crusades against pagans in Northern Europe, and in between these campaigns he fought against English forces on behalf of King Charles.

In 1396 he fought in another Crusade alongside French, German, Hungarian, and English forces, this time against the Turkish army in Eastern Europe. The Christian forces were defeated, and Boucicaut was captured and later ransomed. He fought the Turks again in 1399 at Constantinople, where he successfully ended the Turkish blockade of the city. Upon his return to France, Boucicaut founded an order of knights called the Company of the White Lady of the Green Shield, which pledged to defend all noble ladies and children. Boucicaut continued to lead military campaigns for his king until he was captured by English forces at the Battle of Agincourt in 1415. He died in captivity before the ransom could be raised.

CHAPTER 4

CRUSADING ARMIES

E urope saw many wars and conflicts during the Middle Ages, and knights participated in nearly all of them. But what made a crusade different? Crusades were initiated by a Catholic religious leader, usually the Pope, and were considered Holy Wars, sanctioned by God. Each crusade began with a call to arms by said religious leader and was designed to take land from non-Christians or to protect Christians from non-Christian invad-

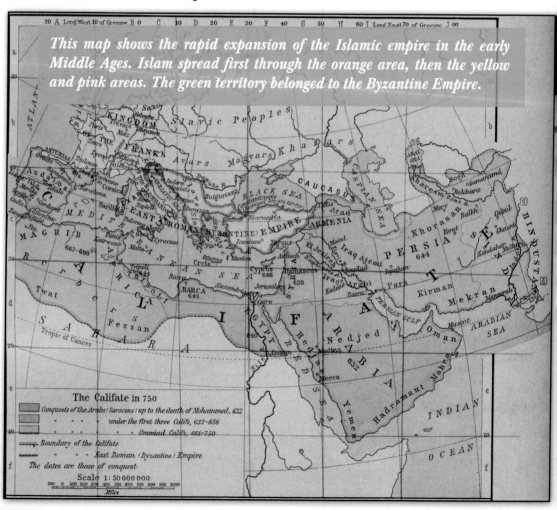

This map shows the rapid expansion of the Islamic empire in the early Middle Ages. Islam spread first through the orange area, then the yellow and pink areas. The green territory belonged to the Byzantine Empire.

The Califate in 750
Conquests of the Arabs (Saracens) up to the death of Mohammed, 632
  "   "   "   under the first three Califs, 632-656
  "   "   "   "   Ommiad Califs, 661-750
Boundary of the Califate
  "   "   "   East Roman (Byzantine) Empire
The dates are those of conquest
Scale 1:50 000 000
Miles

ing armies. Catholics in medieval Europe believed that they were recapturing lost territory or rescuing land that rightfully belonged to Christians.

A MATTER OF FAITH

Although crusades were waged against several different opponents, the most famous crusades were directed against Islamic Turks. Islam began in the seventh century on the Arabian Peninsula, and an Islamic empire quickly spread across the Middle East, North Africa, and modern-day Spain and Portugal. This area included Jerusalem, the Holy Land for Jews, Christians, and Muslims. Most of these regions were part of the Roman Empire before its fall and had been primarily Christian before Islam spread to the areas.

As the Roman Empire fell, warring factions divided the land into many different kingdoms in the west, each with their own political leaders, and the Byzantine Empire in the east. The Christian religious leaders were also divided by different religious philosophies––the Roman Catholic Church in western Europe and the Orthodox Christian Church in the Byzantine Empire. In 1071 the Turks conquered part of the Byzantine Empire and started preventing Christians from traveling to the Holy Land. Catholic and Orthodox Christians believed that it was their religious right to make pilgrimages to the Holy Land, so the Byzantine Emperor turned to the Catholic Pope for help.

In 1095 at the Council of Clermont, Pope Urban II called for a crusade to churches under Catholic authority. Urban's speech also makes it clear that violence among knights in Europe had become a serious social problem. The structure of the feudal system and the political tensions in Europe had created a class of warriors who were continually fighting among themselves, often destroying property and killing innocent people in the process. Urban's speech called for knights to turn their aggression and their weapons to a holy cause, so that the peace of God could be maintained at home.

THE FIRST CRUSADE

The armies of the First Crusade embarked in 1096. The main fighting force was comprised of nobles from France, Flanders, Germany, and Italy, with their pledged knights and infantry. These forces were divided into four armies, each lead by a noble who had been appointed by Pope Urban. The largest army contained almost 10,000 fighters, approximately 1,200 of whom were knights. These armies met at Constantinople, the capital of Byzantium, where they received supplies from the emperor and promised that they would return all recaptured land to the Byzantine Empire.

In their first major battle against the Turks, the Crusaders recovered the city of Nicaea. Obeying their

Fifteenth-century depiction of the siege of Jerusalem during the First Crusade

oath to the emperor, they handed the city over to Byzantine forces and continued toward Jerusalem. The next leg of their journey took two more years. Despite their promise to the emperor, many nobles broke away from the

THE KNIGHTS TEMPLAR

After the success of the First Crusade, Christian pilgrimages to the Holy Land became increasingly popular. However, the journey was still not safe as armed bandits frequently attacked travelers on the roads. In order to protect pilgrims, as well as his kingdom, the King of Jerusalem established one of the most famous orders of knights—the Knights Templar.

The group was originally housed in the Temple of Solomon in Jerusalem and so they took the name Poor Knights of Christ and the Temple of Solomon, usually shortened to Knights Templar. These knights took religious orders, effectively becoming fighting monks. They dressed in white with a red cross to mark their religious vows. This order became an important fighting force in the successive Crusades, as well as a strong economic force in Europe. To pay for the cost of their knights, the order developed some of the first banking systems. This included a system of credits for pilgrims traveling to the Holy Land. Before leaving Europe, pilgrims deposited their valuables with a Templar bank and received a letter of credit. When they arrived in the Holy Land they took the letter to another Templar bank and received the equivalent amount of money, minus a fee. This made travel much safer because pilgrims were not carrying valuables with them on the road.

The Knights Templar wore a red cross on their clothes and sometimes shields to signify their holy mission.

which wetted the European appetite for the fine goods that could be acquired through trade. Arabic mathematics, science, and philosophy influenced intellectual developments in Europe. Although the age of knights was over by the sixteenth century, their exploits continued to affect European culture for several centuries.

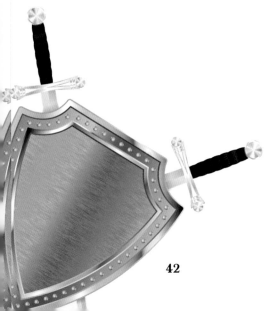

GLOSSARY

armor A covering worn by knights as a defense against weapons.

chivalry Ideal qualities in a knight that include valor, courtesy, and respect for women.

courtly Polite and refined.

feudal system A system of social organization in which one person promises service and loyalty in exchange for gifts and social advancement.

gallant Brave and spirited.

garrison A body of troops stationed in a fortified place such as a castle.

ideology A belief or philosophy in life that guides an individual or group.

joust A competition between knights.

knight-errant A knight who is not pledged to a lord. *Errant* means "wandering" in Latin.

lance A long, speared weapon used by knights in jousting and in warfare.

maiden A girl or unmarried woman generally considered pure in the Middle Ages.

mail Flexible armor of interlocking rings.

mêlée A mock battle between groups of knights.

mercenary A warrior who is paid to fight by whoever needs him.

nobility An upper class in medieval society.

pagan A person who is not Christian.

page A boy in service to a knight, often before becoming a squire and then a knight.

pilgrimage A long journey to a religious or sacred place.

pillage To violently steal money or goods.

sacred Devoted or dedicated to a religious entity or purpose.

serf A medieval peasant or servant who is only permitted to leave his or her lord's land without the lord's permission.

shield A broad piece of armor held by a knight in defense against weaponry.

squire A knight in training.

theology The study of religion and religious beliefs.

troubadour A traveling poet and singer.

vassal Someone who has pledged their service to a lord.

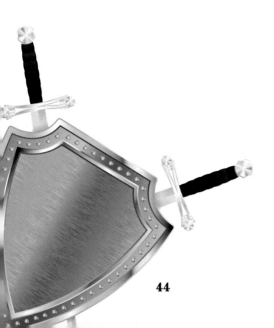

FOR FURTHER READING

Bouchard, Constance Brittain. *Knights in History and Legend*. Buffalo, NY: Firefly, 2009.

Davis, Tony, and Gregory Rogers. *At the Joust*. New York, NY: Yearling, 2011.

Ganeri, Anita, and Mariano Epelbaum. *How to Live Like a Medieval Knight*. Minneapolis, MN: Hungry Tomato, 2016.

Gies, Joseph, and Frances Gies. *Life in a Medieval Castle*. New York, NY: Harper & Row Publishers, 2015.

Gies, Joseph, and Frances Gies. *Life in a Medieval City*. New York:, NY Harper & Row Publishers, 2016.

Gies, Joseph, and Frances Gies. *Life in a Medieval Village*. New York, NY: Harper & Row Publishers, 2016.

Helstrom, Kraig. *Knights*. Minneapolis, MN: Bellwether Media, 2012.

Hepplewhite, Peter. *Knights*. Mankato, MN: Arcturus Publishing, 2014.

Jeffrey, Gary, and Terry Riley. *Crusades*. New York, NY: Crabtree Publishing Company, 2014.

Kallen, Stuart A. *Life During the Crusades*. San Diego, CA: ReferencePoint Press, 2015.

Mersey, Daniel, and Alan Lathwell. *The Knights of the Round Table*. Long Island, NY: Osprey Publishing, 2015

Nicholson, Helen. *Knight Templar: 1120–1312*. Oxford, UK: Osprey Publishing, 2004.

Nixon, James. *Knights*. London, England: Franklin Watts, 2013.

Park, Louise, and Timothy Love. *The Medieval Knight*. New York, NY: Marshall Cavendish Benchmark, 2010

Riggs, Kate. *Knights*. Mankato, MN: Creative Education, 2011.

Saxena, Shalini. *The Legend of King Arthur* (Famous Legends). New York, NY: Gareth Stevens Publishing, 2015.

Star, Fleur. *Castles and Knights*. New York, NY: DK Publishing, 2014.

Websites

Because of the changing nature of internet links, Rosen Publishing has developed an online list of websites related to the subject of this book. This site is updated regularly. Please use this link to access this list:

http://www.rosenlinks.com/WAW/knight

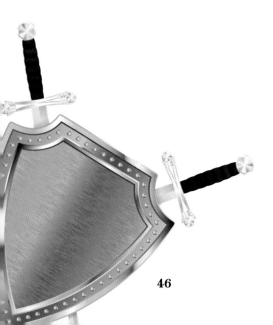

INDEX